D0899727

First Edition
1 2 3 4 5 6 7 8 9

Copyright ©2018 by Max Brett
Design by Jennifer Boyd
Photography by Nicholas Cope

Library of Congress 2019934383
Cataloging-in-Publication Data
ISBN 978-1-948587-00-6

PANK Magazine | PANK Books

To purchase multiple copies or for book
events, readings and author signings contact:
awesome@pankmagazine.com.

NOR
DO
THESE
MAX
BRETT

[PANK]BOOKS

Introduction

Each piece of writing was spurred by 30 unique two-concept prompts (color and complex scientific term) randomly selected by a bipolar third party (to whom this book is dedicated) over a 30-day period in the early fall. Under the terms of the exercise, I had 30 minutes to write each day based on the words assigned. I wrote principally from a cubicle, but also from other enclosures, in fluctuating states of mind, various pressures encroaching. In this way a collection of words was assembled. The terms, of course, could be considered a sort of conscious collaboration and motivator; the hand of the third party.

Initially, three people participated in this iteration of the exercise: A Colombian who would write short musical compositions to the prompts (whose relationship with the third party troubles me intensely); the third party (a life partner of sorts, at least at the time of writing), who would draw based on the prompts; and myself. The third party and the Colombian abandoned the exercise, the latter for a series of performances in Bogotá.

Contents

DAY

chemostat/strawberry

Minas Gerais-born Paulo contemplated the use of the chemostat in the industrial production of ethanol, which his company produced at what could accurately be described as an industrial level, it being the No. 2 producer of ethanol in the No. 1 ethanol-producing country in the world, and he reflected how murky, in fact, the production process was, as the actual usage and mechanics of the chemostat was, to him, completely incomprehensible, representing the limits of his intelligence, really, and then, the use of a machine and -- and -- the chemistry -- or what he assumed to be the chemistry -- would necessarily be opaque to someone like him; his degree was in finance and his purview was the management of this Brazilian ethanol company's increasingly complicated, characteristically tortured financial process, the kind of thing that eventually would end up as a source of dull pain, with attendant staff cuts, the shutdown of certain noncore vanity projects that would make the CEO inaudibly and then audibly grumble during earnings calls with biting analysts, who would ask why he pursued those "vanity" projects, and he would say those analysts did not see the "big picture" or failed to grasp the "large" or "dominant" "narrative," and that they were obligated and bound by their jobs, if you could call those jobs jobs (jobs jobs jobs jobs), well, the CEO wouldn't enjoy the kerfuffle, in fact he'd be streamed or irked or riled or displeased about it, but it would be in monotone, his displeasure would almost be a constant and controlled influx, a nourished, unaltered rate in a vacuum or a tank or a safe enclosure and watched-over container, and then he would have to look at the numbers, and to make them his with control and precision he retained not a small degree of mastery over; well, it was his precise skill set, you didn't get to be where he was without some degree of aptitude, not to the CFO level, without a sort of fluency in book-balancing, detail-orientation, person-   or people-management. (And, let's not deny the degree charisma played here, there were elements at times of a personality contest in the CFO dance.) Paulo ate strawberry after strawberry from a container of many strawberries and the unusual yellow and bright summer light on a polluted day through the window cast his bright white face in a deep, reflected, uniform red.

biofilm/melon

SUBJECT is shaking. SUBJECT's eyes closed. SUBJECT seeing behind closed eyes (is he seeing?) colors. There are peaches, melons, strawberries. There is burning red. SUBJECT smells melons. SUBJECT's eyes open.

SUBJECT's headache is intense and situated in left side of head. SUBJECT's pain is somewhere between swelling and radiating and acute. SUBJECT dresses after brushing teeth, rinsing mouth with mouthwash, washing face, drying face and scalp with towel. SUBJECT has swollen tongue; sores. Lesions at tip and sides of tongue. SUBJECT is dehydrated; excessive consumption of alcohol has amplified dehydration and tongue is an especial source of discomfort for SUBJECT. Teeth of SUBJECT are covered in a thin, abundant biofilm. Jagged, mossy plaque on teeth; battered tongue feels like "it is scraping against asphalt/mosaic."

SUBJECT undergoes commute to air-conditioned facility.

SUBJECT would be well-served to visit dentist at some soon point. [NOTE: Remind SUBJECT of necessity of dental visit.] SUBJECT is at risk of Pontiac fever, risk of which is exacerbated by low or lax quality of maintenance in air-conditioned facility. Illness, should SUBJECT contract it, passes on its own without serious implications. It is not contagious.

SUBJECT types at work terminal and is increasingly troubled by inescapable actual invisible reality of billions of cells sticking together on every surface SUBJECT has touched and interacted with and even seen throughout present day and each day before it and every day SUBJECT experiences subsequently. Vast and invisible universe of microscopic life in world of SUBJECT is troubling enough that SUBJECT does not work optimally through morning.

decoherence/glitter

As Leni Zeh was at the apex of labor pains she shut her eyes and attempted to defang the ripping and tearing and the life to come by visualizing cobblestones outside Dankwarderode castle, glittering after a brief spring downpour, and Heinz-Dieter Zeh was out, covered in fluid and blood, screaming. Two months later, Heinz-Dieter Zeh's perfectly fat baby arms and legs kicked outside his control, most likely, as he (perhaps) was able to visually focus on the mobile above his crib; he seemed to be keenly watching it. Or so Leni and Karl believed, adoringly. But H.D., thick, perfectly normal, helpless, inert nugget of Lower Saxon manflesh that he was, was working through psycho-physical parallelism and the absolute unimportance of securing or defining or assigning a fixed address to the macrorealm, just the silliness of any such concept. H.D. could really use a bit more breastmilk, he felt, as this was heavy lifting. When the allies torched Braunschweig on 15 October 1944, and the Aldstadt was kindling to the flame, 12-year-old H.D. was scared and thrilled by the thermodynamic irreversibility.

positron/quartz

" '____! ____!' the thrilled, perhaps aroused positron trilled, hurtling toward the petrified electron. A climax of vengeful pleasure was the last thing the positron was able to feel before Valhalla.

"For you see, my darling, the electron had lived an empty life -- a false and empty life, unfaithful to itself and those it loved. It bears repeating that the worst of it was the self-deception. The story illustrates the necessity of truth, or the necessity of seeking the truth, or perhaps only the singular importance of living an existence faithful to the pursuit of one's own comprehension of self. The positron, by way of contrast, had experienced an existence charged by the ceaseless quest for self-knowledge -- a noble position for our brave position to take, a courageous position -- and self-knowledge could be said to be the only thing we can attain; an aspiration we have the ability to realize. For to know anything outside oneself is an exercise in futility -- ambrosial futility, as pursuits without meaning can become, somehow all the more attractive because they mean nothing, are nothing, cannot be anything ... My dear, please don't cry. You are very mature and you are prepared the important lessons imparted by the actualized positron and a dovish and minor electron."He picked up the bottle from the quartz countertop and poured the dregs into his glass. Downing it, he waited for further reaction from the coffee grinder.

carotenoids/blond

His hair is luminous, silky and strong, white-blond and falling over his shoulders. The bangs are unorthodox, lightly feathered, and cover a wall of a brow.

The white of the skin, a sort of matte white, unbuffed ivory without any trace of yellowing, is almost as white as the whites of his eyes, which are very, very white. The skin of the face is smooth and without pores, shining, and also luminous, greaseless. The irises are blue, cold, with a sort of permanence.

The skin is fortified by a diet comprised almost entirely of carotenoid-rich fruits and vegetables. He does not remember that last time he felt sick. His nose is large and prominent and strong and his nostrils flare to suck up air.

His ears -- just visible under the blond deluge -- are perfect seashells from a black, pebbled beach in the Pacific northwest. They are edible. They are dimpled at the lobes and appear pierced.

The lips are full and sensual and never have dead or dry skin. They are lubed, also reflective, capable of imparting tremendous pleasure, of conveying enormous disdain.

The teeth are white and straight and small. Baby teeth. The tongue is red and long and thick.

He is wide-shouldered and has thorough, though not imposing, musculature. A blue cockatoo rests in his cupped hand. The parrot seems to smile and is at ease. The parrot occasionally nibbles his thumb gently. In the other hand is a spiny succulent.

His buttocks are firm and exist in a realm without gravity. They rise up to greet one.

He does not have public hair. His penis looks veinless. The foreskin is immaculate and keeps his bell end from being desensitized.

He is the most formidable accountant at the accountancy conference.

half-life/taupe

A bag of red lentils is washed thoroughly, with damaged lentils discarded and any soil and/or refuse tossed. They are then covered in water and brought to a vigorous boil. At this point, big spoonfuls of turmeric and many thin slices of ginger are added. When the water level has cooked down and when the lentils are tender, oil is heated to a shimmering heat in a separate nonstick pan, about 100 cumin seeds are added to the oil, and as they begin to pop, loudly, mirchi or other spicy ground red pepper and ground, dried coriander, to taste, is added to the hot oil. Stirred in its frying pan once, the hot spice mixture is poured directly into the lentils, and stirred until incorporated.

Turmeric and the cooking process render the lentils an intense, saturated yellow, but the addition of the spices -- a baby-fist of hot pepper, an eyeball of coriander, brandy snifter of cumin seeds are used, as is advised (once again, adjusting for taste) -- what is left is a taupe mass of pulses.

The daal is improved over days as the individual spices meld in a unifying harmony unique to each rendition of the dish. The spiciness of the daal has no half-life, it experiences no diminishing of force or weakening. It gets more and more spicy, almost inedibly spicy, intolerably spicy, burningly and powerfully spicy, growing exponentially in what is known as "doubling time."

Gastrointestinal anguish, tremendous gas, and an inclination toward diet variation limit the possibility of consuming one pound of this daal before its inevitable decline. It is therefore often necessary to freeze the daal so as not to lose it to spoilage.

And in the freezing, doubling time as it relates to spiciness becomes almost a tripling or quadrupling time -- defrosted, the daal reserves are almost blindingly spicy, enough to make a person sweat and often necessitating the use of yogurt, chopped, fresh cilantro and bread as accompaniments.

inertia/purple

This limenitis arthemis astyanax, vividly purple (atypical of the species, though not unknown, prized and rare) was far south of its territory and was delighting in dry heat and penetrating sunlight. To an human observer, the flight evoked delight or joyfulness, as the butterfly rapidly and purposefully changed altitude, speed and velocity in the brilliant morning, when evasion, escape and self-preservation defined its movements.

The collector of butterflies had been, for close to a lifetime, a devoted observer of this flight, and often such observation had the duration of lifetimes, for the collector, and charged the collector's existence, and made the collector feel immortal. On this occasion -- again, as it had been for the collector for months now, an unbearable length of unprecedented, recurring, passionless bystander-ism -- the appearance of a butterfly in flight meant nothing. Dense, thick melancholia had taken the place of definition. Too thick, inertia without end.

basal body/bone

"Fertility awareness-based methods of family planning aren't foolproof, or even advisable, in some cases. It's a matter of diligence and monitoring ... but given your aversion..."

"My allergy..."

"... to birth control, and whatever it does to you, and I don't have your records at hand, because I am a cat, a feline who happens to be a doctor to humans, here in this alley with you, and I don't have access to your records, because I don't keep paper records and don't have a fax machine because I am, as you can see, as you've known throughout your treatment and our relationship, a cat -- anyhow, monitoring your basal body temperature might be part of your answer."

"I'm willing to try."

Two other kitties ran down the alley. The doctor and the kitties let forth ominous meows, echoing, prolonged warning meows, until a neighbor drenched them in water. Recovering her composure, the doctor continued:

"You're going to want to use elevated levels of basal

body temperature as signals -- keys -- to avoid unprotected sex. When you are fully relaxed, or at rest -- that's your basal body temperature. A slight increase in temperature could -- I emphasize could -- indicate that you are on the cusp of ovulating. You'll be most fertile before ovulating. Before. There's literature on this. Alcohol and stress make basal body temperature difficult to accurately monitor. You also likely want to use this in tandem with the cervical mucus method. Research that as well. I would still advocate condom usage."

"Alright."

"To the matter of my..."

She opened a can of Wild Planet Wild Albacore tuna for the cat doctor. The contained flesh was white as bone. The doctor proceeded to tuck in.

white hole/sapphire

"Hypersurface," "Schwarzschild coordinates," "gravitational singularity," "White Hole" and other possibly related terms were written or etched with various media on the wall of the stall of the bathroom he used. None of the usual profanity and not inexpertly lettered.

He drove around hulking, tremendous redwoods stretching into an azure sky, not quite successful in obliterating it. He approached the drive-thru-tree park, which had squarish cuts in the trunks of trees large enough to drive cars through. He approached the first slowly to savor the novelty of driving through a tree, but the moment, or instant, that preceded his passage crawled endlessly, through eternity, and he kept seeming to be approaching the entrance and not yet reaching it, and he could smell the wood and feel the air and continued to edge closer and he was still on his way, near admittance, but never crossed the threshold, not so much trapped as infinitely unable to reach his destination, and this was taking years, it felt like years, and might go into oblivion.

abiogenesis/maroon

Beer filled the maroon bottle on the assembly line. Its cap was affixed and the bottle felt whole. The bottle was a vessel and its purpose was to contain. It has been forged with sand combined with soda ash and limestone and its makeup was the makeup of the earth and it had been transformed and was alive.

During shipment, the bottle brimmed with the sense of possibility, grouped with five of its siblings in a cardboard holder in a truck laden with its extended and endless family.

After its fluid was consumed, and it was discarded in the recycling bin in the apartment and then in the larger recycling bin downstairs, there was a feeling of dislocation. Dislocation was gradually replaced by dread.

The bottle came to know the process. The vast community of blighted can and bottle collectors would pick it and its fellows out of this bin and put them into a mobile cart. They would then be taken to the recycling facility north of here, at the market. And that way led annihilation and extinction.

It was said that entering the collection slot meant

a brief, sharp, excruciating crash. And on Friday morning when this bottle found itself in the bin downstairs with its kin, it heard a recycling or refuse truck, affixed with some sort of crane devise, lift up the remains of its broken fellows -- some still existing, conscious, screaming --- and pour them into the vast bed. From that initial crash of pain and death, some believed that reincarnation took place -- a muddled process of melting and transforming, and re-forming with pieces of oneself and others and returning to existence to again be a vessel, to again contain and be used, before being again crushed and remolded, cyclically, endlessly.

There was also the starker possibility of holocaust; ceasing to be, of a mass graveyard and end, of a dump.

As the bottle waited inert for the coming Friday, when it, too, would become part of the line or line segment of existence common to all bottles in this part of the world, it wondered if the sand and soda ash and limestone that made it up were not themselves alive, whether they experienced abiogenesis. It was worth contemplating.

neutrino/gold

The Neutrino GoldVictor 1670TyutR4 Running Shoe is designed for the compulsive runner who worships fast and lives speed. Informed by the specifications of legendary biathlete Zorg Bjorg-Borg, a WhiteHoleImpact © midsole (described by *Runner's Universe** as a "marshmallow on top of a pillow on top of a California King") ensures an impactless, frictionless footstrike. Bursae © cushioning make strides Shar Pei-soft. A synthetic FootWeave © upper hugs the footside/foottop for fullsome footfeel and the SkinSmoke © saclike inner lining does what it sounds like it does. A CreamPink waffle outsole says "Fuck You" to God.

Beam-in hard and dial-up that doodad.
#DialUpThatDoodad

Available in maroon or sapphire.

Runner's Universe is a Pegasus publication. Pegasus is part of the Giraffe Group, a subsidiary of FortyCo.

bacillus/coral

They were exploring the somehow simultaneously turquoise and flaming orange bacillus-shaped pillar coral off the northern coast of Jamaica. It was a thoroughly romantic Caribbean diving vacation with extended periods of erotic contact for the computational biologists, who had heard about how transformationally beautiful these trips were from marine biologist friends at marine biologist gatherings. Marine biologists are excessive romantics with the enthusiasm of children and the computational biologists over wine had had a difficult time believing that diving was so great, that coral was so wonderful to see, that the ocean was so marvelous to feel around them and that breathing underwater was somehow transformational. Being data-driven analytical model-building spreadsheet-worshipers with disciplinary grounding in visualization, biophysics, computer science and genomics, to name just a few fields pertinent to their specialization, marine biology had a quaint and vaguely pejorative quasi-spiritual association, and its proselytizers were the credulous and converted.

anoxic/ruby

A subsidiary of PotGlobalAshFertCorp, the -traded potash and fertilizer conglomerate, pumped "carbon-siphoned, PotGlobalAshFertCorp-safe fluid byproduct" its representatives and legal team and in-house chemical team assured provincial and national regulatory bodies was safe (up to the most recent provincial and national regulations, which predated the current center-center parliament in by a number of decades) into the lake in the small town where the PotGlobalAshFertCorp subsidiary was -- is -- headquartered. The PotGlobalAshFertCorp subsidiary did -- does -- employ almost all of the population of the town and surrounding communities, up to and including members of the aboriginal groups, for which PotGlobalAshFertCorp received an "Up & at Them: Aboriginal Empowerment" award from Business Concerns, a trade publication.

Ruby-red, strawberry pipes extended from the subsidiary plant and into the lake water, where the discharge led to a short-lived and catastrophic algae bloom, rendering the lake anoxic and killing off the local fish. Media attention that ensued was briefly outraged and then distracted.

Hawking radiation/lava

Yakov Zel'dovich was a cantaloupe-headed Jewish Belarusian physics genius. Thick, black-framed glasses rested on his bitter-melon nose. His full, thick, sensual, glittery lips were known as the most sensual in the Institute of Applied Mathematics, and earned him the nickname "Glitter Lips." His lips were also recognized as sensual by colleagues at the Sternberg Astronomical Institute. The reader will probably have reasoned (correctly) that those in his field were predominantly thin-lipped.

Zel'dovich arguably gifted the great English physicist Stephen Hawking the concept of Hawking radiation, as this Hawking radiation concept came after a visit to Zel'dovich and Alexei Starobinsky in 1973, when they essentially sat young Hawking down and explained the phenomenon. Zel'dovich would die in 1987.

Hawking's compliment after his time with Zel'dovich is too good not to quote: "Before I met you," meaning Zel'dovich, "I believed you to be a collective author, like Bourbaki." This would fly over the head of any reader not familiar with Nicolas Bourbaki, the collective pseudonym for a 20th-century mathematics troupe. Hawking was saying that Glitter Lips was brilliant enough to be mistaken for multiple geniuses simultaneously and collaboratively at work solving impossibly difficult problems.

A 2014 commemorative stamp shows Glitter Lips intense, with a restrained grey suit and darker tie, and three medals clamped to his chest, one likely being the Kurchatov Medal, the highest honor in nuclear physics in the USSR, though this must be wrong, as the three medals appear identical.

Behind his likeness on the stamp, that is to say in the background, a hazy sun descends into lava.

isotope/lemon

Glenallen Hill, manager of the Albuquerque Isotopes, a minor league baseball team, is a noted arachnophobe. During his time as a slugger in the major leagues, he had an outrageous and terrible nightmare in which he was compelled to take an invitation to tea with an enormous lemon-yellow spider. At the large maroon table in the dream, the spider was so at ease, so comfortable in the cream-colored lobby of the luxurious hotel, as she lifted a cup of hibiscus tea and sipped it underneath razor-sharp fangs. Glenallen Hill, seized by fear-inertia in a high-backed chair, felt unable to extricate himself from the social obligation with the spider. And then Glenallen woke up screaming and flailing and fell down a flight of stairs.

plasma/cream

The unicorn sat on the bar stool, slowly drinking its whisky. Its mane, all the colors of the rainbow, contrasted sharply with the fresh cream-colored tone of the hair all over its body, and its prominent, horsey face. Its eyes were cut sapphires. The glittering threat of its pointed and long horn was dazzling.

It sat there on the maroon stool, with its rainbow tail spilling over, with the cracked upholstery at -- this was coincidental -- The White Horse, with its maroon interior and exterior walls and its cracked clientele.

Roger sensed that the Unicorn didn't like to talk and that it wasn't because the Unicorn was rude or that the Unicorn was supernatural or that the Unicorn felt superior because it was mystical. The Unicorn was self-contained and couldn't bear small talk, clearly. You don't mind bar at The White Horse for however many decades as Roger had without some sense of customers, whoever or whatever they happened to be.

The Unicorn was tired of the chase. It was being hunted by a group of investment bankers, it had been for weeks, they were relentless. This group had individually and collectively hunted man-eating tigers in India, wearing the masks they told you to wear on the back of your head but that did nothing. They had lost a senior VP on a hunt. And then elephants of both Asian and African origin, big Kodiaks out in Alaska.

John D. Rockefeller Jr., collector of spectacularly bloody and inhumane looking unicorn-hunt fine-silk-and-silver-thread tapestries displayed in the Cloisters, knew the intense pleasure the wealthy experience hunting down and destroying unicorns.

These bankers felt they also knew it, or could come to know it.

This current group of bankers had recently applied for transfers from the Deutsche Bank mother ship in Frankfurt to New York to hunt the Unicorn. So why was the Unicorn at The White Horse in a banker-rich district? Did the Unicorn want a fight?

Roger didn't know. The plasma screen was showing the Mets and the Rockies. The Mets were surprisingly good this year.

quark/royal blue

After the acrimonious endpoint of a long relationship, the royal blue quark thought it would never find love again. And then it met a crimson lepton. Their possible fundamental symmetry was fundamentally symmetrical. R. Foot and H. Lew looked on approvingly.

"Royal quark ... blue," she told the confused Baja Fresh cashier. She would not move out of the line until her demands were met. To avoid eye contact with the clearly deranged customer, a line chef stirred a maroon pot of beans.

"Quark! Quark! Quark! Quark" went the hungry and lonely mallard, desperate for tourist bread. Those legs were kicking frantically under the royal blue lake. "That duck has a speech impediment," said the Parks and Recreation employee.

The Athletic Bilbao-Barcelona match was a quarking quarker of a royal blue spectacle of a madhouse jamboree (and so on) ...

"Quark and Royal Blue" is not a palindrome. But what if it were? ("Imagine" begins to play...)

The blonde, handsome lawyer in the royal blue polo

on the Citibank-blue Citibike saw the car moments too late. Everyone on the block turned as the impact broke his femur audibly and crunched his ribs, smashing and stabbing into internal organs and killing him quickly. His dead sapphire eyes looked into a searing blue sky. A bystander with great calves finished smoking a cigarette.

The landing page of the website for Quark Pharmaceuticals features a moderately handsome young actor in a cream labcoat in the role of a doctor. Looking at a maroon-colored liquid in a glass beaker -- possibly a fake urine sample from a fake offscreen patient who in this false reality has something wrong with their kidneys -- he stands in front of a graphically created royal blue backdrop. He's lighted from underneath by a canary yellow light. It's worth repeating, on and on to oneself, that marketing is big in pharma.

"Quark is a leader in the development and discovery of novel RNAi-based therapeutics," the website reads.

betahemolysis/magenta

The fleshy, rounded buttresses of her throat were inflamed and magenta, striated and swollen, as her pharyngitis intensified and sharpened and her voice began to go.

Her impetigo had also worsened. Rafting, she had cut and scraped herself on a rocky outcropping and at the time had felt a pleasurable exhilaration, not knowing whether she was going to be recovered. Days later thick bumps had appeared on her legs and then burst and she was covered -- her legs were covered -- in magenta cores that crusted over, eventually. They were very itchy and took great effort not to scratch.

Perhaps most uncomfortable was her erysipelas, from the Greek, also known as "St. Anthony's fire," which were on her toes and hands. The magenta rashes were well-demarcated. She was also having trouble sleeping.

Her tongue was covered partly by a white film, but the rest was especially red, sort of a fuchsia red, and she was feverish. It was uncommon for a person of her age to contract scarlet fever, but it was not unheard of, as her doctors had told her.

Vaguely hungry, she warmed something on her small

stove. Her cat licked itself repeatedly with its hard, purplish-red feline tongue and let out a cat-sneeze. The cat regarded her briefly before staring at the ceiling.

dark field/grey

When and how the rats had developed a cohesive plan of escape and a collaborative organizational structure was unclear, and was remarkable, as many had spent so much time in solitary confinement. It was likely at some point after the scientists had all died and stopped performing experiments and stopped feeding them. Led by a large, grey female with a broken tail (Lucinda), they moved in the windowless, timeless freezing cold light of the modern polygon pharmaceutical laboratory/facility, releasing each other from their cages, sniffing about, moving swiftly over steel, with purpose, through corridors, over and under tables, avoiding the ashy corpses of the scientists. There were so many they appeared a single great squeaking calico mass with Lucinda in the lead, squeaking direction and guidance, squeaking encouraging squeaks to baby rats, squeak-counseling scared rats, squeaking calm to the overly excited ones.

Outside the laboratory was a dark, endless field, singed near the entrance of the main campus of the building but scorched further on. The sky was an unvarying nickel-cobalt. The noise was an unbroken silver static cackle.

horizon/bone

The final model of the anticipated fall/winter collection of AA Arturizth was a 14-year old, two-metre tall, raven-haired, grey-eyed, magenta- lipped, milk-skinned Croatian who had also been pursued by rival designers for their own final walks, to no avail, because Marina Matic's representatives weren't clowns or new to this and knew Arturizth meant much more to Matic -- much more to the agency -- than the others.

She had eaten a single, ethically picked royal blue blueberry in the lead-up to her walk, and had wept for hours beforehand, purposefully, knowing how thrashed it would help her to look, how consumed. The walk was so important. This was her most important walk. She kept repeating this.

Conceived as an homage to Battle of Magenta in the Second Italian War of Independence, the show featured models in Insurbres tattered rags and ended with her as an indomitable Zouave. Not a Zouave in the strict French light infantry sense, but a spiritual Zouave, stepping on the skulls of vanquished or shitting Austrians, splitting those skulls with a "pop" and a lava effluence with her tall, thin heels. Arturizth had almost had to psych her into wearing those heels beforehand, flicking her harder and harder with a metallic, reinforced fingernail and silently hating her.

As she began her walk a medium-length gasp raged through the audience. Her ankle-length robe-tunic was essentially chainmail with polished bone shards up to 8 centimetres in length attached so that she appeared a totemic porcupine, with the bones swinging freely, stabbing her from time to time. She slowly moved down the runway, stabbing herself inadvertently. Nearing the end, she stepped out over the crowd and continued to walk, levitating. She kept walking, suspended, as the walls broke open and she continued her walk on toward the horizon until she was just a speck, then gone.

cosmic inflation/plum

The plant's development was quick.

An enormous and empty field in the U.S. Southeast was cleared. Bulldozers did most of the work and trucks pulled away the refuse. Large machines orchestrated the foundation, dug into the red clay earth. This work took place over many acres. There wasn't much to the area before the German automobile company started to conceptualize its factory here, lured by tax incentives, personal appeals of politicians, letter-writing campaigns, abiding dirt-cheapedness. And up the factory grew, immense beyond immensities in these quiet reaches of the southeast, multi-tiered, multi-complexed, nearly a penitentiary of machines that built machines in windowless environments. The machines were serviced by unionized autoworkers who had human managers who oversaw them. Over the first years, the plant underwent something that could be described as a cosmic inflation, or what here amounted to a sort of cosmic inflation; a rapid birth from nothing, seemingly without end.

Communities sprung up around the plant peopled by the workers who worked the lines and the managers who managed the workers and the other executives. Residential developments with homes of slight variation ripped serpentine-style outward, devouring former plantation-land. Swim meets transpired on thick, muggy summer says, with parents standing alongside the pool, cheering. Marching bands accompanied football team games and basketball games. There were rare suicides and no school shootings. Boys were concussed, drank by the river, fought, studied, had conservative haircuts, went to church; female children played field hockey, studied earnestly, did not have short haircuts, whipped people inadvertently with encouraged, lengthy ponytails, looked up to their fathers. Marriages endured, soured, ended, renewed. Dogs happily lived in the moment and protected their apes. Cats cleaned themselves quietly. A deer was hit by a car occasionally. Weekend fishing trips, weekend high school sporting events. Flatscreen plasma televisions. Microwave bacon.

When it was decided the plant would be shuttered (commodity prices, lower demand for this particular German automobile brand), and that thousands would lose their jobs, the community was, understandably, gutted and helpless, and the families -- particularly lower-wage families -- began to move away, painfully, out of necessity, and it contracted.

Months after the workers had all been dismissed, a group of college students decided to break into the automobile plant to observe what was once a busy place at total inactivity. The lawns were already overgrown. Most of the machines were removed, but documents were everywhere, almost as though they'd been thrown into the air. Large rectangular computer monitors, not worth the cost of removing. Calendars, timecards. Coffeemakers. It vibrated with isolation. There were other things: a small tin soldier depicting a Zulu warrior; a 19th-century quilt adorned with snakes; bones of mammalian origin, seemingly a prehistoric armadillo of some kind; a large bowl of what once must have been plums, now rotten and decomposed, bubbling over the sides with purplish fluid; a raven or crow whose wings had a magenta sheen, flying across a main assembly hall, caw-ing at nothing, or perhaps at the students.

oscillating universe/seashell

A team of creators have collaborated to know without margin of error that the candy bar has an initial, exponential burst of flavor, upon first bite, that renders the mouth helpless, a spectator to the wonderfully violent, surging moments of creation -- the creators understood this from the case studies and the chemistry and the testimonials of the subjects who had tasted Prototype Oo. The tasters of Prototype Oo felt, afterward, that they had never before tasted, that they had never before existed, and to understood themselves to be, post-bite, both travelling and building "universes" at once. Prototype Oo is a layer of _____, covered in 99% _____, wrapped in 0.55 mm microlayers of with just an almost imperceptible _____, laden or shot through or charged with proprietary chemicals. Its exact composition was the most guarded proprietary information in the Belgian multinational. The mouthfeel of the bar alone had taken years to develop, as had the tonguefeel. Rather than look like chocolate coming out of the as-yet-determined final wrapper, the surface of Prototype Oo had the oil slick iridescence of an abalone shell -- detractors of this final choice said that the team wanted to suggest the cosmos, as if they had created the universe.

The case or study subjects who had eaten Prototype

Oo, however, had begun to kill themselves off. The sensation of pleasure and of everything-coming-to-being-out-of-nothing that the candy bar gave off to each taster was followed by what the creators called the "big crash." At first a subtle sense of the great expanse of the flavor, the limitless pleasure of it, compressing, minimizing, becoming more compact, hot and bright, unbearably so. One child under observation going through this withdrawal -- withdrawal? -- screamed before bursting her head into the one-way mirror, alarming the behavioral psychologists observing her, "Implosion into singularity!!!"

Project "Oscillating Universe" wasn't without cost, but the senior vice president believed it had traction across demographics.

fruiting bodies/gold

I drove the Fiat to the town square to pick him up; Giorgio had told me he is a freelancer, a freelance photographer and writer, and would pay me to allow him to take pictures of me and Bella as Bella and I looked for tartufi, murdered in English as "truffles," in the piney woods. As arranged with Giorgio, he stood beside a statue honoring someone, some figure in the history of my country, such things are often the permanent occupants of town squares. Vest, expensive camera, a vacant smile, impractically long hair useful for grabbing, clothes he incorrectly believed were appropriate for a hike.

I drove around the square staring directly at him, and he was clearly confused, as he knew by my very direct look that I was his escort, the "gruff-and-uneducated-but-fundamentally-decent-and-even-somewhat-noble-in-his-way-I- think" truffle seeker-outer, but my face was expressionless, which was likely scary, being 20-something and in a "foreign country" and guileless and trusting and never-before-challenged and never-before-criticized and without any imagination as to how someone might desire his death and, likely, any command of Italian or any knowledge of the country beyond superficialities.

I kept driving around and around the circle. Staring. He was clearly becoming disconcerted, alarmed.

Who would read him? I am not totally divorced from the modern world, though I shitted in the woods and looked for mushrooms or fruiting bodies with my dog Bella, because my father and his had done this and it was what I was doing. I was, of course, a factotum in the process of people paying supplemental fees for extra truffle shavings on their pasta, but somehow the idea of a documentarian celebrating the inceptive point of that excess was a real irritant. I thought of the office worker somewhere, who would see his post and click on it and try, to no avail, to drown out the printing copier and the cubicle where he'd probably put a postcard or multiple postcards depicting scenes distracting him from that which was in front of him, or not in front of him. He'd hope for something else. He would read of the shaggy truffle hunter and think of Piedmont and escape.

I left him in the square. Bella and I would go on to have a good day. They were usually good days.

sepia/gas

This particular giant Australian cuttlefish, or sepia arama, is seen as beyond the control of the Australian government. The Santos gas groundwater contamination that ravaged cuttlefish breeding grounds in Port Bonython off the state of South Australia in the Upper Spencer Gulf is thought to have somehow made the animal monstrous and savage, but introspective, highly literate, even a bit pretentious, flashing all the while, an ability much-noted in the species.

white hole/mist

The mist in the San Francisco park fell over, an opaque white moment in city time, deep and impenetrable.

The bipolar monster relative imagined something gold and cream and magenta and wild and then was confronted with air conditioning and duffel bags. "I'll gladly be down here," he said.

He was speaking to the dust-and-grime-covered-inanimate BART train.

panspermia/lust

Years in, the rancid and suffocating quality of the culture led to the conclusion that accidental panspermia was an undeniably compelling and righteous concept and likely the only possible explanation for that which was all around me -- that a unknowable precursor extraterrestrial race, fat from technological innovations, sassy from conquering, wheezing in motorized conveyances in ships that nimbly traversed galaxies, had dumped a load of hot summer garbage, really pungent effluence, on the earth, which composted or rotted (same thing?) and began creating microorganisms that had given birth to the environment here and was responsible for the slothful, bored, dead things that walked the halls, befouled the three-stalled bathroom, erupted into drunken reverie whenever the opportunity presented itself, celebrating nothingness, giving no love, and addressed the material and immeasurable joy and blessing of existence with tremendous, callous inactivity, indifference, certainly improper worship at the miraculous state of affairs. Looking upon one ambitionless, puffy, half-bearded drudge wearing a shirt like a tablecloth was enough to cause the abandonment of hope, the death of lust or desire, and to embrace, or concede, the futility so married to or one with mortality. Yes, accidental panspermia made more and more sense, when you looked with clear eyes and concentrated, a near-impossible task through the current hangover. Used condoms, avocado skins, Kleenex, habanero bases, butter wrappers, banana peels, basil stems, garlic skins, water-bloated tea bags, beer bottle caps, yellowed and mucosa-laden cotton swabs, band aids, clumps of cat hair, animal hair, eggshells, ashes, molding mushrooms -- or equivalent, strange, alien waste matter -- was definitely responsible for humankind, which, in turn, was destroying the waste it was born out of.

element/green

In his last months in the cracked, noisy apartment in the dangerous, often abandoned neighborhood, I visited him. His partner had returned; he answered the door his eyes were bloodshot, his nose was shiny and red; he was high and a little drunk. He wore a single sock -- one of her green socks -- and grey sweatpants, despite the heat, which was uncomfortable and unseasonable. His things were in disarray, shifting.

"She ironed my pants," he said -- mournfully? resigned? bemused? -- taking the beer I had brought out of my hands, walking inside. Some beans were on the boil. Plants on the sill above the sink looked wilted, a yellower green. Disheveled was probably the word.

We were quiet for a period. We heard glass shatter outside, someone cursing at a woman. It was silent for a while, and then the ripping sound of a motorcycle. It would go like this -- minutes of silence and then a metal shriek or human pain shriek or something.

He went to the bathroom. He came back. Then he stared at his monitor. I decided to walk outside, into the hot, damp night, surrounded by palm trees, stepping over a neon green pool of auto fluid of some sort, looking in vain for stray cats, listening to distant screams, animal scuffles, smelling the smell of mold or fetid -- but not quite fetid -- plant growth and death, and excrement from a variety of species, and the mountains were around and people lived there but it was often invisible at night, and the sky was starless.

ion/burgundy

Just as atoms in their neutral state may be a different color than in their ionic state, so his placid, relaxed face became disgusted, furious, angry, contorted, octopus-like; this large face, normally ashen, tinged yellow, with slack skin, turned a deep and impassioned red color, and seemed to regain the force that he once so easily relayed, imparted, inflicted and used or employed or deployed. He spent time forever in transit between coastal cities. They were not impossibly far enough away from each other to split his life between, which is precisely what he did. This meant a lot of printouts, a sore-assedness, a struoture denuded of musculature.

He pounded Diet Cokes and also had a sweet tooth that favored the chemical and lent itself to the abuse of a variety of pastries, from Hostess cakes to Fruity Pebbles to Big Hunks to Snickers and Mars bars to jelly beans from the terminus to tarts and chocolate cake, to almond croissants to cookies of all size, shape and description. He allowed that the genre of sweets was as big, to him, as the known universe, and he loved them so. He often had crumbs of some kind on his otherwise clean dress shirts and ties. Not slovenly, just a bit untidy, and even then, acceptably.

Years after having no dreams whatsoever he kept

having these terrible dreams, black holes of constricting terror, or perhaps white holes of never reaching a point, of inert purgatorial constant progress, with no gratification.

Light absorption by metal ions gives gemstones their pleasing, shocking, delightful color. He thought of this for no reason wandering a wine rack full of Burgundies.

emerald/nectary

South of the shining long swaying emerald-leafed branches of the weeping willows to the west of the hulking granite (likely granite) or grey stone monster bunker of the Museum of Jewish Heritage was a lavender patch about the size of four Japanese sedans arranged in a square. Occasional passersby ran their hand through the blossoms and nectaries contained at their peril, for the lavender patch was a favorite area of congregation for the few remaining fuzzy saffron bees that themselves delighted in the oasis west of the museum and south of those willows, sobbing and wailing, distraught. North and east of them, under one of the structural wedges that projected from the museum's west wall, a painfully thin, shirtless man who in no way appeared destitute, as his hair, pants and skin were clean, practiced tai chi, protected from the hot hot 2 p.m. sun, right now cutting into the layers of the skin of many of the European tourists wandering here and there.

East of the lavender patch, two couples were guided in a Lamaze class by a dirty old crone in tights and a loose shirt.

Out on the water, a massive sailboat pitched in the churning waters. The captain had decided to ram the coast guard. The coast guard captain, hardly unaware of the approach of a massive, wobbling sailboat, manned the gun at starboard and took out his rabid colleague, not before clipping screaming blonde Northern Europeans on holiday.

A fins and backs of a pod of killer whales crested the water, on the hunt for great white liver, maroon and delicious. Rare to see them this far east.

hydrostatic equilibrium/bronze

The mastiff (or whatever gigantic breed of dog he was, and it was a he, his balls swelled) slobbered calmly outside the Citibank ATM kioskish storefront, waiting for his master to complete his withdrawal. His coat was a mixture of coal with bronze flecks or highlights.

Half the books in the bar that had been styled to look like a library were unsold textbooks on hydrostatic equilibrium. The bar's owner only paid for the shipping, and it fit with his sense of humor to think of a person going to the shelf to read while at the bar and finding a big academic text on hydrostatic equilibrium.

The publishing houses were briefly convinced that hydrostatic equilibrium would take off as a genre. Careers were broken.

The banker with bronze clasps, bronze skin and golden/ bronze hair got on at Wall Street and disembarked at Fulton Street. She was covered in glass and didn't make eye contact.

A person in glasses furiously underlined her novel's text--as the train jostled, she missed her book and landed on her leg, where, after a pause, she began an impossible illustration of the northern lights over the

U.S.-Canada Border.

Her watch was made in China by counterfeiters directly contributing to the destruction of the textile sector in Nigeria.

An advertisement for a tennis tournament features a Russian blonde with blonde-gold-bronze ponytail a-flash in the midst of a backhand, and it read, "she won't look back." In the background there is an Asian banker in a maroon tie, a striped blue shirt and a teal suit.

The person in front of me has copper hair.Maybe bronze. Her nine-pronged earrings are definitely made of copper. Or bronze. Her ring is a loaf-shaped black diamond set in bronze.